SAMTHOLOGY

SAMTHOLOGY

A Tribute to Sam Hamill

SEATTLE POETICS LAB • SEATTLE, WASHINGTON

Published by:
Seattle Poetics Lab
Seattle, Washington
www.Splab.org

Samthology: A Tribute to Sam Hamill
Copyright 2019 Paul E. Nelson
All rights reserved.

ISBN: 978-0-578-49606-1

Printed in the United States of America

Cover design: Ian Boyden
Interior design: Gray Dog Press www.GrayDogPress.com

Acknowledgments

The *Samthology* would not have been possible without support from Kim Miller, Middlepoint Press, Martín Espada, Ian Boyden, Cate Gable, Lyn Coffin and Stanley and Resha Sabre. We are grateful for this support, for the use of Cate Gable's photographs and for the example Sam Hamill gave us: how to live life in service to poetry.

Contents

Introduction

"America? Crumbling empire," growled the master from his kitchen table strewn with pipe paraphernalia, a sake bottle, and glasses from the evening before. "Not much we can do about it.[1]"

But then, of course, Sam Hamill—poet, publisher, translator, editor, and mentor for so many—went on to talk about how essential it is to passionately pursue a life of moral value in literature.

"I've never been a patriot. Patriotism seems to me a disease of the soul. I prefer to think of myself as a working, functional humanist. In my own way, I love my country. But it's a love hate relationship that's often abusive. To look at the violence in American is to really look into our soul and blaming the politicians is not excusable, it's not an answer. We get the government we deserve."

In the final chapter of his life, Sam continued to inspire, rage, write, and animatedly converse about the state of the world; his home was the meeting place for friends, writers, and artists of all stripes as it had always been. After the death of his beloved wife Gray, he chose to live out his days in Anacortes beside the Salish Sea, with a view of Fidalgo Bay and Mt. Baker—Koma Kulshan, the name given to this volcano by the Lummi people. In the long tradition of Tu Fu, Li Po, and Basho, Sam was rooted in and attentive to the natural world as if it too were a lover.

He liked nothing better than to treat visitors to a sushi dinner with plenty of sake at Sakura in Burlington, or a meal of oysters and Malbec at Nell Thorn's in La Connor. (The walls in both places must surely be saturated with Hamill's special brand of raw, vibrant ideas about the state of literature, poetry, publishing, and politics.)

---

1 These quotations are taken from an interview Cate Gable conducted with Sam Hamill at his residence on October 5, 2016.

Still working to his last days, Sam's final volumes—*Ce que l'eau sait* (a bilingual edition published by Le Temps des Cerises, Paris, 2016) and *After Morning Rain* (Tiger Bark Press, Rochester, New York, 2018)— contained poetry as powerful and relevant as any he had written; with the wisdom he gleaned from looking back over his life, he acknowledged his coming death:

> Here I once made love with a woman I adored
> while a lonely figure watched from bluffs high above,
> and the gray implacable tide drew away
> to meet the gray implacable sky.
>
> Our cries—love or death—were drowned
> by the cries of wandering gulls. Now a year
> has passed. And still he is there, watching
> from the shadows, sighing the sighs of the sea.
>
> Memory, like waves. Stained with the salts of desire,
> a shoreline creature talking fear away,
> I go on confessing to the water, understanding
> only that the final sentence is death…[2]

Contemporary political circumstances tempered and refined Sam's lifelong commitment to peace and right action. In 2003, after turning down George W. Bush's invitation to the White House, Sam created Poets Against the War, both the movement and, with the help of Sally Anderson, the publication: an anthology of 30,000 poems by 26,000 poets. These efforts put Sam squarely in an international spotlight and reinforced the fact that poetry still matters.

"We have to find some kind of moral bearing if we're not going to live with a sickness of the soul. For me that has been the transformational experience of devoting much of my life to working on behalf of nonviolence and literature. The only realistic solution to the current state of the world is individual responsibility. There have

---

2 The final stanzas in section 6, from "Destination Zero," by Sam Hamill.

always been great artists who addressed the issues of their age. I don't aspire to be a great artist—I aspire to be a working artist. My highest ambition was always to become a minor poet: I think that's a pretty high ambition. And the odds are that I won't make it."

"All of this literary prestige-stuff that goes around is nonsense. I can't imagine anyone fifty years from now getting up in the middle of the night to look up a poem by John Ashbery. I don't see it happening."

Though Sam may have scoffed at literature which he felt was produced too often in the service of the ego, he did not deny the legacy of the authentic voice. In fact, Sam was brilliant at reading aloud his favorite poets in their own voices and inflections, part of his insistence on the primacy of breath. Students of Sam's often heard his adage, "Poetry—stick it in your ear." For him, poetry was not meant to be an object on the page but was a vital living creation made of and with breath.

"When I was teaching poetry I used to write on the blackboard the last lines of Rilke's 'Archaic Torso of Apollo'—'You must change your life.'—Do you think he was kidding? The study and appreciation of poetry absolutely must change your life; it has to question your values and your value systems and your priorities. If poetry doesn't change your life maybe poetry isn't for you."

Poetry made Sam's life. From the age of three when he was adopted and raised by a Utah farming couple, Sam managed—after drug addiction, petty theft, jail time, and a stint in the Marines—to find his way to poetry; and, via Albert Camus's essays, to a life of pacifism, literature, and Zen practice. Sam's writing was influenced by 20th Century poets Rexroth, Pound, Olson, Williams, Creeley, Duncan, Carruth, and Levertov. Sam was co-founder of, editor and book designer at Copper Canyon Press from 1972-2004; he is the author of 17 volumes of original poetry; four collections of literary essays; and the translator of major Japanese, Chinese, Estonian, Greek, Latin, and Vietnamese poets and writers. His own writing has been translated into more than a dozen languages.

Sam was awarded fellowships from the National Endowment for the Arts, the Guggenheim Foundation, the Woodrow Wilson Foundation, and the Mellon Fund; he was honored with the Stanley Lindberg Lifetime Achievement Award for Editing and the Washington Poets Association's Lifetime Achievement Award, among others.

About poetry, Sam has said, "We're all invisible poets. We'll all be forgotten in ten minutes." It is difficult to imagine Sam's legacy will suffer that fate.

Cate Gable
Nahcotta, Washington
March 2019

For the Samthology Team:
Paul Nelson, Ian Boyden, and Lyn Coffin

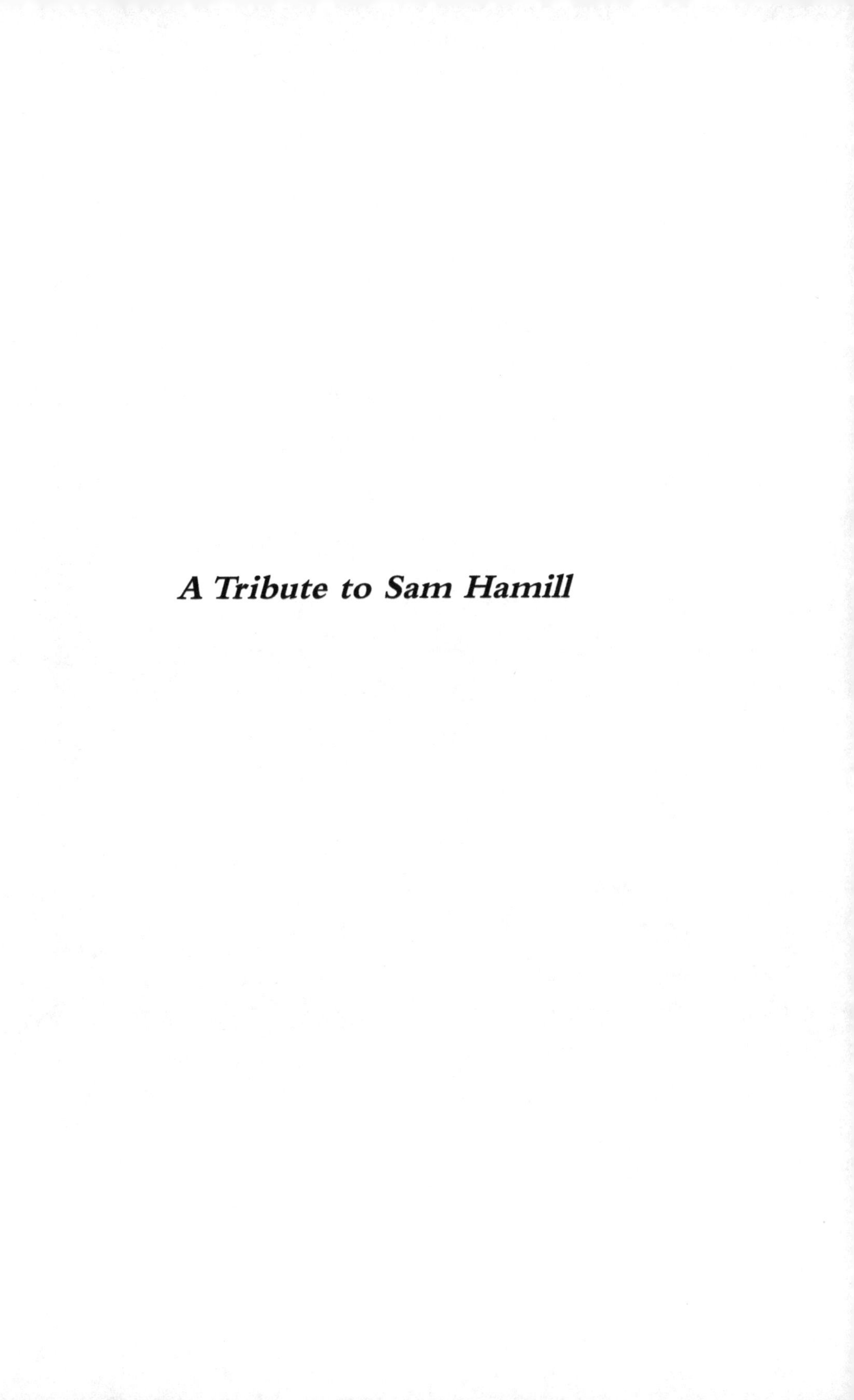

A Tribute to Sam Hamill

Drinking At Sundown

To Sam Hamill, on his 74th birthday
We're drunk again tonight
and I think of us in France
in Dordogne at sunset
We're drinking red wine by the river
I mention Augiéras, whom you've never heard of
I think of us again, this time in Brittany
where I'm beginning a new life, where you won't come visit
It is sunset again, on the beach at Montsarrac
and barnacle geese call
from behind the horizon
And I think again, as we're drinking too much
of all those places where we will not be together
because your health
will not allow it
because reality
will not have it that way
I think of us as kids in the darkness
who imagine worlds and tell each other stories
to stay awake
borne on the edge of the world
on the feathers
of their whispers
As they promise each other
never to grow old.

Anacortes, 9th May 2017

www.versopolis.com/poet/169/alexis-bernaut/poem/1702/buvant

Buvant Au Couchant

Pour Sam Hamill, à l'occasion de son 74e anniversaire
Ce soir nous sommes encore
saouls et je nous imagine en France
en Dordogne au couchant
Nous buvons un verre de rouge au bord de la rivière
Je te parle d'Augiéras, que tu ne connais pas
Je nous imagine encore, en Bretagne cette fois
où je commence à vivre, où tu ne viendras pas
C'est toujours le couchant, la plage de Montsarrac
et les oies bernaches crient
derrière l'horizon
Et j'imagine encore comme nous buvons trop
tous ces lieux magnifiques où nous ne serons pas
parce que ta santé
ne le permettra pas
que la réalité
ça ne marche pas comme ça
Je nous imagine comme des gosses dans le noir
qui s'inventent des mondes et se disent des histoires
pour ne pas s'endormir
portés aux bords du monde
sur les plumes
de leurs chuchotements
Tandis qu'ils se promettent
de ne jamais vieillir.

Anacortes, 9 mai 2017
Alexis Bernaut

學柯 Study The Axe Handle
for Sam Hamill

To study the axe handle
is to study the forest,
how trees stand,
and how trees fall,
and how to cause their falling,
and what it sounds like,
when one falls into one's own shadow
by another's hand.

To study the axe handle
is to study Lu Ji,
third century poet and author of the *Wen fu*,
who was wrongfully executed for high treason,
and who once wrote:
> *Things move into the shadows and vanish.*
> *Memory returns in an echo.*

Moment by moment.
Axe cut by axe cut.
Telling truth by truth
as the foundation of one's art,
even if it is also the foundation
of one's own wrongful execution.

The seedling just sprouting
has already fallen as a giant tree,
one limb is already the handle
of another limb's demise.

It has fallen at the edge of a name
of a child who has fallen,
who is moving into shadows
filled with echoes
and the memory of vanishing,

Everything can lead to everything
but it doesn't.
Each leads to each singularity
in all of its impermanence.

Ian Boyden

s a m i m m e m o r i a l

r y w b p a s t a a o f r l w f
a o i l a r l r s n u i e i i a
i u n o p r i a w d t s a n t l
n r d o e a v y e a o h d e h l
r r o m r n e y l g n i i s t i
a e w i a g r o l e f n n a h n
i p a n n e s u a d i g g n e g
n a b g d s o u s c d b y d s r
i i o a y t n s w a a o o o o a
n n v s o a a e h m l a u u u i
g t e b u n s d e e g t a r n n
s e t l r g i t a m o s l v d
t d h a d e l o t b b s o o o
r k e n a r v l c e a o u i f
e i o k u i e i r r y w d c
a t r l g n r k a t n e y e
k c c y h e   e c   o s o s
s h h a t   k   t u m
  e i s e   e   a r i
  n d   r   r   r   x
                s   t

Getting to Know Sam

Swarmed by poets vying for your attention
you picked my poem from other offerings
and entered my world

The buzz stopped
they watched your lips
move down the page

"Send a few poems
to Copper Canyon"
you said quietly

You read what there was
in my asking eyes, smiled
and went to get some water

Nootka Rose

I always knew
Nootka Rose
by its wild name

It was native—
the land bloomed
with its thorns

Its pink flowers
and a red fruit it bore
still flare against the blue sky

Dumb Luck

Let's start with gratitude
measured by stone
that almost made it to paradise

If it hadn't been for carnal pleasure
the stones would have moved
to destination zero

When poets marched
against the war
bombs rained on Baghdad streets

As dumb luck would have it
roses flowered that summer
in cradles as deep as the craters of bombs

Seattle, December 12, 2018
Leszek Chudziński

Letter from Boston

Sam,
The third renovation in a row the crew walked off today.
Nothing gets finished, "just abandoned," but the job leaves splinters.
Lifting a stout at *The Plough,* your name came up.
Tim read a poem about quitting this hardhat economy
by a guy from the Tetons: frozen fenceposts and the usual—
snow, hardened compost, woodsmoke,
a line from time to time that missed the beat
because we stay too long within the rhythms of the trades.

The body beside me sleeps like a machine.
Breath noises, inward murmur, a moan within the dream.
Romance the illusion of the mirror, Cocteau's door to hell,
who cares about Eurydice?
                                    We can't ever quite come to rest.
In a photo of Auden's face cigarette smoke blurs all those creases,
a river's unraveling away from rope.

I won't describe the face I saw tonight on the subway.
Hours later I'm still confused, and ashamed.
We're anonymous enough out here, but this face
charred by all our poisons—I forced my eyes to believe
we were born in the same place, drink the same water,
run a palm across the same chrome and granite.
In the rattling seats, most of us show no longing.
A creased brow and I look toward the window
where my own face blackens, passing underground,
brake-lights flowering on the tunnel wall.
When the train lurches, I get out and walk into the city
—a thin Vietnamese in woman's slippers
shivers in the draft below a vent.
Not far away a heaven's made from turrets and old tiles—
the perishable order of doorways, a man asleep on a stoop
where someone's hand placed a withered carrot.

Past shadow and streetlight at the quarry entrance,
slate and granite veined, whorled, chopped, routed
and eroded by a stream, or shoe and wheel
these roads of lichen, algae, oldest mosses, oak and bowers of elm.
In Munich, Aschenbach, before he fell in love
as the boy ushered him toward death
passed a place like this and smelled the coming war.
Headstones harvested here line up blank.
To me, a young and foolish optimist, they're shouting,
"We resist, we resist, we resist you."

I was a boy full of milk and loved the wind
veering down a street a mile from here
the summer my hand took form from an arrow,
pines fanned one another in a field.
My forearm sore from the bowstring,
the first shots fell into New Hampshire,
but then grinded one after another unlike any bird,
twanged against a straw bag of bullseyes.
A hawk above the boughs brushed small loops of haze.
I'm not sure why I wrote you this letter.
I walked in black fields and animals called me a man.
"Nostalgia," Rexroth said in that way he has
of instilling syllables as if carving them on a maple
whose leaves in the clear basin beside his camp
sing the history of every word. But it's not that.

Try this—I'm driving with the family on a typical Thursday.
Passing a lake, I want to have a look.
Grandmother objects, but I pull over anyway
and the noises stop, no ripples—
a birch stand fills with dusk, sky turns to chalk.
I set the bow—how green this lichen.
Fieldstone walls have served a hundred families,
each more indifferent than the rest,
but I draw the bow, can't waste a shot,

arrow feathers leave my hand,
the shaft disappears then, bone white,
arcs over the hawk's tail
and falls back down to me,
craning my neck to watch.

Quincy, MA, 1979
Michael Daley

Blasphemy

For Sam Hamill

Let the blasphemy be spoken: poetry can save us,
not the way a fisherman pulls the drowning swimmer
into his boat, not the way Jesus, between screams,
promised life everlasting to the thief crucified beside him
on the hill, but salvation nevertheless.

Somewhere a convict sobs into a book of poems
from the prison library, and I know why
his hands are careful not to break the brittle pages.

Martín Espada

Milosz and Hamill

Nakagawa means the middle of the river, Sam tells me
in Paris scribing kanji on a napkin at the round table
of the Japanese café.

The middle of the river is where the rocks are tossed up
by spring freshet, their sad faces left bare, or where
deep currents carry them home.

It's either the unattainable or the edible earth,
the tussle of two great minds—one who knows the secret,
if it exists, and one who will.

Cate Gable
2016, Paris

Coast Chronicles: Loose in Paris with a Fugitive Poet

Sometimes the words come freely,
sometimes we sit in silence, gnawing on a brush.

Sam Hamill, translated from Lu Chi

In Utah, the nice farm lady picked up a rascally small boy from the orphanage and told him, "Your father has a dog for you." When three-year-old Sam Hamill got out of the car, he looked up and down a tall skinny guy with a dog and said, "That's not my father and that's not my dog," establishing definitively and for all time his beingness in the world.

As Sam now says, "I have a BS detector with no off switch." This has been, as most gifts from the Gods, both a blessing and a curse.

A Poet's Roots

I met Sam perhaps forty years ago. I was a little MA graduate from the University of Washington and Sam (with then wife Tree Swenson) was the co-founder of Copper Canyon Press, situated in Port Townsend at Fort Warden. I think I bumped into Sam at some poetry gathering there and mentioned that I'd taken a poetry book and was meaning to send money to the author but hadn't yet (and probably didn't). As I vaguely recall, Sam pointed a finger at me and said something like, "You suckered so-and-so out of his dough!" (This is what Sam might call, "One Finger Zen.")

Poet, pressman, editor and publisher, translator of Japanese and Chinese masters, philosopher, Zen Buddhist, crusader against domestic violence and war—Sam, like a comet, has a long trail behind him of social justice actions. He puts his heart-mind-and-body on the line wherever he must and has at every step of his life.

Always on point, Sam was one of the first poets I thought of when I started my critical thesis for my recent MFA. (I wanted to talk to other writers about what they thought was happening in the world and whether they felt poetry/poets still had a viable role in the public discourse.)

Despite a tough life on the farm in Utah—he was often beaten— Sam was also raised with the poetry of Dylan Thomas, Robert Service, Keats and Shelley poured into his ears by two very literate parents. He was an outsider from the beginning and had mostly "brown friends." As he says, "I always felt like a brown person." Though his parents, who were not Mormon, sent him to Mormon church so he could "learn to get along" that doesn't appear to have done much good; it probably accentuated his otherness.

Sam became in many ways the active conscience of a generation of poets of the 60s. At sixteen and a heroin addict on the streets of San Francisco, he'd wander into City Lights Books in North Beach and read poetry in the basement. He counts Kenneth Rexroth as the reason he wised up/cleaned up.

They sent him back to Utah to straighten out but picked up for a drug charge there, Sam says the judge told him, "You can either go to jail or join the military." Big of heart and mind though small in stature, Sam of course chose the Marines, the most machismo branch of the service. Sent to Japan, he realized quite soon that his values required him to be a conscientious objector; but he managed to stay in uniform long enough to leave with an honorable discharge and, therefore, the means to an education.

Sam in Paris

As far as I can tell, Sam has either known, edited or published and probably gotten drunk with every major American poet of the last century, and most of the major foreign poets as well. He has stories

about Robert Creely, Denise Levertov, Adrienne Rich, Marilyn
Hacker, Judy Grahn, June Jordan, Hayden Carruth, William Merwin,
Carolyn Kizer, Jack Gilbert, Tom McGrath, Jim Harrison, Czeslaw
Milosz—he could write the underground version of who's who of
American poetry. He's read his poetry across our nation, and in Italy,
France, Germany, Greece, Latin American, and Asia.

But let's skip an enormous chunk of Sam's story—please imagine,
film-style, not just calendar pages falling like leaves but being
blow-torched off the wall— and begin again last week when Sam
arrived in Paris to celebrate the bilingual publication of his most
recent book, "Ce que l'eau sait"— what the water knows. (These
poems are selections from Sam's *Habitation: Collected Poems*, Lost
Horse Press, 2014). The book is a not only a masterpiece of poetic
achievement but a beautiful object d'art. (You can order the book
here: http://www.letempsdescerises.net/?product=ce-que-leau-sait)
The cover holds an exquisite Morris Graves drawing of a small
animal with bushy whiskers and squinty eyes. Not unlike how Sam
presents now with the wispy white beard of a sage and curls at the
back of his neck. When he laughs, which is often and loudly, his eyes
disappear.

Last night we attended a poetry reading at Sam's publishing house
in Paris, Le Temps des Cerises, which translates as cherry season, and
is, in fact, right now—the time when cherries plump up on their
trees. This is also a song, originally written by Jean-Baptiste Clement,
which became the revolutionary anthem after the struggle of the
Paris Commune in 1871. Cherries metaphorically hold the meaning
of sexuality and the fullness of life but in the song also become drops
of blood falling through the trees. It's an apt name for the work of
the press being carried on by Juliette Combes Latour, the daughter of
the founder.

Sam read with Alexis Bernaut, a good friend and one of his French
translators; as well as Salal al Hamdani, an Iraqi poet and one of Sam's
poetic brothers; and Salal's partner Isabel Lagny. (Salal has had a life

with amazing parallels to Sam's; he was awakened to literature and
became a poet as a prisoner in Abu Ghraib—but that's another story.)

The reading took place on Parisian cobblestones under stormy skies.
I can't help but note that poetry has a veritable place of honor in the
hearts of Europeans. Being a poet is not a career choice, it's a calling
that requires sacrifice of body, mind and spirit. Sam's devotion to
literature and the social justice values he has lived by—his dedication
to stopping violence of any kind, whether domestic or state-
sanctioned—is celebrated in many parts of the world. Sam lives a
solo, contemplative life in Anacortes overlooking the Salish Sea. But
here, surrounded by friends, he is a hero. The last stanza from "After
Morning Rain:"

> And what am I but [love's] solitary
> pilgrim—lost, found, lost again—
> on a long journey whose only end
> is silence before the burning
> of my body, one last moment
> of flame, a whiff of smoke
> washed clean
> and gone with the rain.

Sam finishes his reading and the downpour begins.

Cate Gable

www.chinookobserver.com/opinion/columns/coast-chronicles-
loose-in-paris-with-a-fugitive-poet/article 09365dd4-cccc5323-
bd27-088d47802e48.html

Paris, July 1, 2016: Letter to Sam

You're strapped into your seat
at 38,000 feet of lofty air;
while I stir in Paris on rue Orfila
to sounds of children on the stair.

Your "sparse white beard and haggard
face" (once imagined), last night
over cold sake was grizzled.
You stroke your new beard, test its might

and fill our cups to the level line.
Kanpai! We sip and laugh; we ate
so well. To be a poet means
sitting every day alone. Our fate

is sorting fragments to find
the pearl in hand while the moon
—still teasing—tempts our hearts.
If only I were beautiful, you young;

for now, an empty house
on a hill and a glimpse of the bay
is not enough. What other horizon
falters into view? Truth, you say,

never ends though it's more difficult
to voice as the ship pulls from the dock,
no land in sight, and a phantom
oarsman or woman goads the clock.

The beast slows inevitably, taps
a small tattoo—what have we wasted?
There's doubt at the back of the tongue
where bitterness resides. Haste,

haste, bow down, as every human
thing we've shaped goes to hell,
except for one line scribed on a wall
somewhere: I loved her well.

Cate Gable

The Next Garden

Reading Sam Hamill's Habitation
in my unkempt garden as the sun crests
the roof-line, I watch you descend into the scraggle
of forgotten stalks—brittle, spent, gone
to seed. Last night on Facebook, Sam said
he would like to be in love again,
would like to have a traveling companion to escape
the USA. There were several takers.
I pondered the narrative for the half-life
of beryllium-14 (which is 4.84 seconds). It seems
I don't do love anymore, at least not
with human beings. Your vermillion blaze

bobs above the weedy grail of each desiccated
umbel, erasing my undone chores and botanical
remorse. I forget the day's plans, the incomplete
tax return, the emerging parsley and strawberry leaves
that need the ground cleared of leftover corpses
who were so carefully loved and tended. Once.

Our pact, although forged without words,
is secure in our mismatched hearts (mine is larger
perhaps from too much wanting). And when you transcend
to the next garden, I am on
your wing.

Kim Goldberg

Temple of the Word:
What Sam Hamill Asked of Poetry

Until recently, there were few moments in contemporary poetry
without Sam Hamill's presence. He was an omnivorous participant as
poet, publisher, and editor. There was another role Hamill played—
friend to many, many people (Facebook limited him to five thousand
friends). Hamill reviewed an early book I edited—a compilation of
poets from a Western state whose voices were not widely known.
Their obscurity made no difference to him. What mattered was
the authenticity of their work, their veracity in a world filled with
imitation.

I met Sam Hamill as he was starting on the long journey to
build Copper Canyon Press. Over the years he replied to my many
inquiries, not out of obligation but a desire to mend a broken fence
in our chosen art form: its distance from the reader. I would be
further drawn into his orbit when I began editing a book about
the late Hayden Carruth. They were close friends and Hamill was
Carruth's publisher. I heard Carruth tell more stories about their
escapades than I can recall, but Hamill knew Carruth was unlike
any other. At one point he corralled Carruth and they recorded
him reading thirty-one poems in a barn in upstate New York. That
recording is seminal. Carruth gave many performances but none that
I know of are as arresting as the recording made by Hamill.

Hamill led me to another corner of poetry: his translations of the
ancients—Li Po, Tu Fu, and dozens more. Although *Habitation*, his
collected poems, is staggering, I am most taken by the translations. He
devoted his life to learning Japanese, Mandarin, Buddhist teachings,
and the quiet that comes from such reflection.

> I translate because I want to be in their company—to
> comprehend their art, to learn what they learned and to be
> shaped by their learning, and because I want to make them
> available to others.
>
> SH (Crossing the Yellow River)

Hamill was by no means a quiet person. He could be recalcitrant and insistent, but always for areason. I have spent countless afternoons reading those translations; they help me understand just how finite we are. When Basho comes to a hut on his open road I come with him. That book has taught me how to live alone with few things but my awareness. Hamill wanted this knowledge and yet lived in a time when war and subterfuge made running a press like dancing on a geyser. He could not sit on the sidelines; he could not watch the spiral into Iraq from Port Townsend. He and many others edited *Poets Against the War* and it was predictably renounced by the academy. But today it doesn't look so out of place; we recognize it as testimony.

Sadly, Hamill knew that poetry had become subordinate to words without meaning but he wanted none of it. Nor did the thousands who submitted their poems to be considered. This offended people, and Hamill—a lifelong outsider— found himself firmly planted on the outside. On an April night in 2015 he told me, "In the last ten years, I lost my press, my publisher, my house to fire, and my wife to cancer." He looked at me with eyes that saw no one and everyone. When he got off the plane to give his reading, he sprayed cortisone in his nebulizer. I didn't know if he would make it to the podium that night. But for one hour he held the room captive; they could not move under the weight of his urgency, despite his being on oxygen when I took him back to the room.

Three weeks before he died Hamill wrote:

> I turn 75 in May if I live that long. Final book, *After the Morning Rain* going to Press with Tiger Bark. Very sick. Congestive heart disease & COPD.
>
> ABRAZOS,
>
> Sam

★　　　★　　　★

I am weary of writing these goodbyes. I know a dozen poets
and writers who knew Hamill very well. All of them are wrecked
by this news. Doubtless the press he left behind, Copper Canyon,
has grown to be the most influential poetry press in the U.S. That's
an accomplishment—particularly when you consider it was started
in 1972, when he, Tree Swenson, William O'Daly, and Jim Gautney
left UC Santa Barbara to found it in Denver, CO. They had $500
(an award from the Coordinating Council of Literary Magazines for
Hamill and O'Daly's editing work on the UC Santa Barbara literary
magazine, *Spectrum*), $500 from Gautney's mother, and $250 from the
sale of Hamill's 1947 panel truck. They had no promise of a literary
future but when the UCSB English Department wanted to keep the
$500 award, they left to build a press for poetry, hence the Chinese
character for poetry, <u>shi</u>, which combines temple and word, Copper
Canyon's symbol to this day. Two years later, Hamill and Swenson
relocated the press to Port Townsend, WA. In its long, nascent
journey the press became a marker for countless poets—not unlike
New Directions in the previous decades—until it was the vanguard
of contemporary poetry presses. In 2001 I received a letter from
Hamill—he was worried then about the financial fallout from 9/11.
The press would manage but the September attacks took their toll.

Slowly, I began to see Hamill through the lens of his many
friends, not least of whom was William O'Daly, one of the four
co-founders of the press. O'Daly translated Neruda's later poems
and most recently, Neruda's first book, <u>Book of Twilight</u>—all with
Copper Canyon. Like Hamill, he came to read in Reno and we
have since spent many evenings trying to unravel the great force
that was Hamill. It's no coincidence that Hamill and O'Daly both
became translators. When they met at UC Santa Barbara, they were
studying with Kenneth Rexroth whose translations influenced them
as a model for how to be a poet—how to reconcile the modern
with the old. I think this is what the two men have brought to their
work as poets, as people who see poetry's arc from the early Chinese
masters to the present. To most, this is called perspective: what we
aspire to do in light of our history. A fraction of the ancient Chinese
poets are known and taught in the West. Red Pine's journey to the

headstones of the masters was a daunting reminder of our transitory vocation. Poets rarely live longer than the moments they are given. But it is precisely this perspective that drew Hamill to them. His ego was not in front of his desire to elucidate them. He wanted to know what they knew, to live in their likeness. In this I will not be able to do him justice save to continue reading those translations. Because he was grounded in their experience, their motif for living, I don't believe he expected it would be much different for him. He was indifferent when I asked him how things were? He always shrugged and lit a cigarette.

In the summer of 2015 my wife and I drove to Anacortes, WA, to visit him. He was on the balcony waiting for us to arrive. The poems and journals were scattered inside. A new person had come into his life. He was almost hopeful. We had some wine and talked endlessly about what he wanted to do. *Habitation* had not yet come out. Many fine presses had considered it, but the editors and Hamill tangled. He was no saint but because he was driven to ignite contemporary poetry with this view of its relevance across time, he changed how and why we perceive poetry: it is not an idyll; it is an act of will. Trump has no use for poetry, nor I imagine do his legion of supporters. I could be wrong. Maybe some read poetry but the point is—like Hamill, poetry stands apart from the day-glow events that besmirch our existence. It resonates beyond this time. Hamill's best poems fan out beyond this time.

My friends who published with him tell me his influence was omnipresent. I believe them because Hamill took what I imagined to be poetry's place in this world as the premise of our relationship. It was where we began as two people: with the words of Basho, or Wang Wei, or Sappho. They were fire on our tongues, what we needed to survive *this* unruly moment in time. This required of him a focus not found in most contemporary presses. It required him to lead without approval or conversely, with conviction, until, of course, he no longer could manage the disruptions. If you read Hamill's essays he talks about the unraveling at the press and how his "political activity" in *Poets Against the War* put him at odds with prevailing literary tastes. This attention became a liability for Shambala, his publisher of many years. Before long he found himself on the outside of the very thing he helped create. I was closest to Hamill in this time and watched him writhe in silence. But I remembered what he had done for so many over three decades: given poetry an undeniable presence in this time. Without asking him, I imagine that is what he wanted: to elevate its presence in our lives. How unlike a translator, a publisher, and poet to burnish his reputation as innovator with the quiet work of his ancestors and yet, he refused the other path: singing songs of himself, to paraphrase W.S. Di Piero.

When the Carruth book came out in 2013, Hamill was on a panel with me at AWP. Still weary from the fallout of his many losses, he rose to honor his late and dear friend. I think the other panelists knew that it could have been either man we were talking about: hardscrabble, recalcitrant, serious students of poetry—this was Carruth and his former publisher, Hamill.

What I cannot accept is his absence. In time, the poems, letters, and memories of so many events with him and his friends will comfort. A legacy left when it was most needed. Now we aspire to emulate such justice, to find a way to birth the poem without its attendant repercussions—when only yesterday it could have been outlawed. This was his magnanimous example—how to wake, write, and publish without fear.

Shaun T. Griffin

From *Paragraphs from a Day-Book*

In winter, the produce on the stalls
is rufous roots, dark leaves, luminous tubers,
as if earth voided jewels from its bowels
for my neighbors'
Sunday stew-pots. Concurrent raucous calls
and odors waft among the vegetables:
merguez sizzles in a skillet, fowl
turn on a row of spits. Damp dogs prowl
between wool-stockinged calves and corduroys
Tissue-wrapped clementines
from Morocco (gold from old colonies)
salt fish from Portugal and Spain's
olives and oil; cauliflower from Brittany,
also the channel-crossing mist of rain
down from the northwest coast since yesterday
Thought thrusts up, homely as a hyacinth
wrapped in its bulb like a root-vegetable,
a ninth-month
belly, while the green indelible
pattern's inscribed into the labyrinth.
Lanced into light, it's air's inhabitant
with light and air as food and drink..
A hyacinth, tumescent pink
on the low wooden Mexican chest
confronts the wintry dusk
with informed self-interest.
Leaf-spears extravagantly ask
what idea, still gnarled up in a knot
of ganglions, will break through the husk
shaped at last, recognizable as thought
Trace, on a city map, trajectories
of partially-forgotten words
along the river's arteries,
volatile substance of a sentient world.

Mauve heather crowds the window-grill. The light
lingers a little later, with a slight
vernal inflection. In a moon-glazed vase
bloom yellow freesias, like some rainy day's
brook-bank, in someone else's memory.
Small whirlpools of perception widen, ring
an infant's numinous discoveries
of syllables for animals, toys, trees:
a Lab's thick coat, the dusty birds
in Claremont Park each tardy urban spring,
a stuffed pink leather horse with button eyes.

Grief, pain and sorrow all are "*la douleur*,"
while "*le bonheur*" is simple happiness
which we savored in the hour
seized as the solstice passed
across the heather-misted calendar
whose olive-brown hillocks' December blur
was pierced by the setting sun
as we meandered, *vigneron*
to *vigneron*, well-spring to orchard, stopped
for *Le Monde*, for the view,
pleasure both cumulative and abrupt:
sudden suave vista; beauty we knew
(mist imperceptibly becoming rain)
well enough to recall, while going through
the nuances of sorrow, grief and pain.

Grasp and turn a moment, make it stop,
stand in view, like the freesias in their green
moon with arboreal ribs. A lapsed
monk worked the Burgundian
clay he'd learned, cloistered, to turn and slap,
fire and glaze. While he talked, wet clay dripped
down his bare arms. The moment turns
like clay-slip on a wheel, or burns

with sweetness, like the potter's clover honey
offered to us as we
moved with the wrapped box back into the rainy
winter morning. He'd told me he
read Henry Miller, then re-thought his vows.
Six months out of chemotherapy,
I heard his daughters singing in the house.

What are the engines of that energy?
A path around a vineyard, sandwiches
and Starbucks' coffee
above the Hudson, a long kiss,
five flights of wooden stairs worn slant by three
centuries' footsteps, an old library
book with bracketed sentences
may make the metamorphosis
to firm words from memory's shift and slip
the way the moistened clay
turned and handled on the wheel whirled up
and swelled into the belly of a vase,
and curved out to the flower-implicit lip—
the movement is the potter's, not the clay's:
a flaw, and he aborts it with a slap.

Marilyn Hacker

Homenaje A Sam Hamill

Aunque siguió muriendo hacia la inexistencia su
        última reencarnación
        ocurrió en el período
        Tang.

Su karma lo obligó a transmigrar de la época Song
        al presente (ayer) en
        inglés: el hecho lo
        hacía rabiar, era un
        poeta chino escribiendo
        ideogramas en un idioma
        extranjero, oculto tras los
        mil rostros las mil flores
        de Yang Wan Li, de
        Issa, la rana de Basho
        en arco cayendo en el
        estanque de una casa
        en Seattle, trampantojos
        del agua.

Pudo, lo agradece, en parte remediar las atrocidades
        de Oriente a Occidente
        hasta el presente
        bebiendo ingentes
        cantidades de vino
        de arroz, soju, vino
        de ciruela a la hora
        de los postres con
        Tu Fu, Li Po. Y Li
        Ching Chao: en su
        tumba (actual)
        aparece a petición
        su busto inclinado
        ante la poeta de
        quien se pretende
        para siempre su
        amanuense.

José Kozer

Tribute to Sam Hamill

Although he continued dying toward non-existence
       his latest reincarnation
       occurred in the Tang
       period.

His karma forced him to transmigrate from the Song era
       to the present (yesterday) in
       English: that fact enraged him, he was a
       Chinese poet writing
       ideograms in a foreign
       language, hidden behind
       Yang Wan Li, thousand faces
       thousand flowers,
       from Issa, Basho's arched frog
       falling in the pond of a house
       in Seattle's, illusory water trick.

He could, he is grateful, partly to remedy the atrocities
       from East to West
       up to the present
       drinking enormous
       quantities of rice wine,
       soju, plum wine
       at dessert time with
       Tu Fu, Li Po. And Li
       Ching Chao: in her
       (current) grave
       appears upon request
       her bust inclined
       before the poet
       who forever she intends
       to be her scribe.

José Kozer

Translated from the Spanish by Raúl Sánchez, 5-2-2018

A Devotional for Sam Hamill: Habitude

I walk with a stick and a dog, down river, up, no one can tell me how it's done. A few understand and sing as I pass—the songs are fine—but there are turns in a stream where songs fall apart, they're only melody.

When I was a boy a stove abandoned and filled with crickets was opera—blind kid, twilight blues, the moon coming on blues, and so my first lesson. Later Auden would refine it: "the roses really want to grow..."

Crickets sing a house—find homes—say something.

Oh but the walking blues, songs to poems, walking with a stick and dog.

Michael Cuddihy: Each time breath draws through me,/ I know it's older than I am.

Basho: The journey itself is my home.

Levertov: I saw/ a leaf: I shall not betray you.

Hsieh Ling-Yun: Joy and sorrow pass, each by each,/ failure at one moment, happy success the next./ But not for me. I have chosen freedom/from the world's cares. I chose simplicity.

Dog and stick, down river, up, a crescent moon, poems remembered.

Rexroth: Water/ Flows around and over all/ Obstacles, always seeking/ The lowest place. Equal and/ Opposite, action and reaction,/ An invisible light swarms/ Upward without effort.

Niels Bohr: Everything we call real is made of things that cannot be regarded as real.

Jan Kaplinsi: The sea doesn't want to make waves./The wind doesn't want to blow./Everything wants balance, peace,/and seeking peace has no peace./If you understand this, does it/
change something? Can you be peaceful/even where there is no peace?

Sam Hamill: I'd kiss a fish/and love a stone/and marry the winter rain/if I could persuade this battered earth/to let me make it home.

Kuusisto: I'm filled with tangled string. A look contains the history of man. (Auden) Some days I'm grateful I can't see your faces. Mutual need. Mutual aid. Simple. But even Anarchists are specious. I once introduced myself to Utah Philips, said, in the manner of all young people: "It's a thrill to meet another anarchist." He glared at me. Said nothing. And of course I couldn't see his face. His anarchy had a small "a."

Stick and dog…

Sam Hamill: Fish, bird, stone, there's something/I can't know, but know the same:/I hear the rain inside me/only to look up/into a bitter sun.

Sam Hamill: There are some to whom a place means nothing,/for whom the lazy zeroes/a goshawk carves across the sky/are nothing,/for whom a home is something one can buy./I have long wanted to say,/just once before I die,/I am home.

Sam Hamill: The poem is a mystery, no matter/ how well crafted:/ is a made thing/that embodies nature./And like Zen,/the more we discuss it,/the further away..

Muriel Rukeyser:

We tell beginnings: for the flesh and the answer,
or the look, the lake in the eye that knows,
for the despair that flows down in widest rivers,
cloud of home; and also the green tree of grace,
all in the leaf, in the love that gives us ourselves.

The word of nourishment passes through the women,
soldiers and orchards rooted in constellations,
white towers, eyes of children:
saying in time of war What shall we feed?
I cannot say the end.

Nourish beginnings, let us nourish beginnings.
Not all things are blest, but the
seeds of all things are blest.
The blessing is in the seed.

This moment, this seed, this wave of the sea, this look, this instant of
    love.
Years over wars and an imagining of peace. Or the expiation journey
toward peace which is many wishes flaming together,
fierce pure life, the many-living home.
Love that gives us ourselves, in the world known to all
new techniques for the healing of the wound,
and the unknown world. One life, or the faring stars.

Sam Hamill: Poetry transcends the nation-state. Poetry transcends
government. It brings the traditional concept of power to its knees.
I have always believed poetry to be an eternal conversation in which
the ancient poets remain contemporary, a conversation inviting us
into other languages and cultures even as poetry transcends language
and culture, returning us again and again to primal rhythms and
sounds.

Robert Bly:

Our veins are open to shadow, and our fingertips
Porous to murder. It's only the inattention
Of the prosecutors that lets us go to lunch.
Reading my old letters I notice a secret will.
It's as if another person had planned my life.
Even in the dark, someone is hitching the horses.
That doesn't mean I have done things well.
I have found so many ways to disgrace
Myself, and throw a dark cloth over my head.
Why is it our fault if we fall into desire?
The eel poking his head from his undersea cave
Entices the tiny soul falling out of Heaven.
So many invisible angels work to keep
Us from drowning; so many hands
reach Down to pull the swimmer from the water.
Even though the District Attorney keeps me
Well in mind, grace allows me sometimes
To slip into the Alhambra by night.

Kuusisto:

Life in Wartime

There are bodies that stay home and keep living.
Wisteria and Queen Anne's lace
But women and children, too.
And countless men at gasoline stations.
Schoolteachers who resemble candles,
Boys with metabolisms geared to the future,
Musicians trying for moon effects.
The sky, which cannot expire, readies itself with clouds
Or a perfect blue
Or halos or the amoebic shapes

Of things to come.
The railway weeds are filled with water.
How do living things carry particles
Of sacrifice? Why are gods talking in the corn?
Enough to feel the future underfoot.
Someone is crying three houses down.
Many are gone or are going.

Paulo Freire:

Dominated and exploited in the capitalist system, the lower classes
need—at the same time that they engage in the process of forming
an intellectual discipline—to create a social, civic, and political
discipline, which is absolutely essential to the democracy that goes
beyond the pure bourgeois and liberal democracy and that, finally,
seeks to conquer the injustice and the irresponsibility of capitalism.

Sam Hamill:

Do your homework. Stand for something. Define what you stand for
and live for it and be willing to die by it. It's the same advice I give a
new poet, or for that matter, an old poet. Or a young Buddhist.

Sam Hamill:

You know, poetry's job is to make us feel good. Poetry exists to allow
us to express our innermost feelings. There isn't one role for poetry
in society. There are many roles for poetry. I wrote a poem to seduce
my wife. I wrote a poem when I asked her to marry me. Poetry
got me laid. Poetry got me married. I wrote a number of poems
about Kah Tai lagoon, when Safeway was building that huge, ugly
store down there where I used to love to watch the birds nest. That
political poem, or environmental poem, was unsuccessful because
Safeway built there anyway. And yet the poem has something to say
today, as it did then. And I speak here only of my own poems. The

agenda for every poet has to be different because most of us write
from direct human experience in the world.

Auden:

Can poets (can men in television)
Be saved? It is not easy
To believe in unknowable justice…

Sam Hamill:

Black Marsh Eclogue

Although it is midsummer, the great blue heron
holds darkest winter in his hunched shoulders,
those blue-turning-gray clouds
rising over him like a storm from the Pacific.

He stands in the black marsh
more monument than bird, a wizened prophet
returned from a vanished mythology.
He watches the hearts of things

and does not move or speak. But when
at last he flies, his great wings
cover the darkening sky, and slowly,
as though praying, he lifts, almost motionless,

as he pushes the world away.

[There are turns in a stream where songs fall apart, they're only
melody. But poetry pushes the world outward, then pulls it inward,
with blue-turning-gray clouds.]

Kuusisto:

I'm walking in a yielding air beside my dog, do you understand?
There are no faded hopes beside her, do you understand?
She doesn't care about my eyes.
She doesn't care about the heroes on TV.
She lives without protective lies.
Look at us, we're walking through pitch darkness.

Sam Hamill:

Poetry is one of the ten thousand paths to the Buddha; through
poetry (as various as that word may be), we may find self-realization
and do away with the "I-and-thou" and competitive mind-set that
makes war possible (as well as poetry contests) and we come into a
world of only "we," we-are-oneness" in our struggle in this sentient
interdependent world. To value life requires valuing the cosmos that
makes life possible. How can we actually learn what love is without
learning to fully love this earth on which we stand? —The very dirt
and stone of it. We must protect it from capitalism just as we must
protect those who suffer most from organized oppression. We must
love and resist and rebel.

Stephen Kuusisto

Interview with Sam Hamill
November 1, 2010, at Sam Hamill's home in Anacortes, WA

Paul E Nelson: Sam Hamill is the author of 14 volumes of original poetry, has published 3 collections of essays and 2 dozen volumes translated from Ancient Greek, Latin, Estonian, Japanese, and Chinese. The founding editor of Copper Canyon Press and the Director of Poets Against War. His work has been translated into more than a dozen languages. The latest book is *Measured by Stone.*

Sam just gave a reading at Doe Bay last night. Basically, you read from this and new work, the *Habitation* series, which has not yet been published in book form.

Sam Hamill: In trade form. If you've got a spare $10,000 lying around I got a book for you.

Paul E Nelson: I don't think you've ever told that story about Ian Boyden. You told it last night. We recorded the reading last night so people can refer to the recording, but maybe you could talk a little bit about meeting Ian Boyden and what he did with your work.

Sam Hamill: I discovered his work at an AWP bookfest in Vancouver, B.C. His wife Jennifer told me that my work as poet, translator, printer had been one of his inspirations. He's a studio artist, a painter, scholar of Chinese, and a remarkable artist bookmaker. I wrote the first of the trilogy called, "Habitations," it's basically an ekphrastic poem honoring his unique process of using things like fossilized ear bone of whale ground up into the inks that he makes. I was totally blown away by his work. We met and he sent me some catalog things. I looked at some of his images and I dedicated the first of the "Habitations" trilogy to him, which I thought was just going to be one poem. I realized by the end of it that there had to be a couple follow-up sections. It's a trilogy that I dedicated to him because his work is so profound and so inspirational.

Paul E Nelson: Crab Quill Press.

Sam Hamill: Crab Quill Press.

Paul E Nelson: You realize that it didn't end after the first series of poems, tell us a little bit about that impulse that you recognize there's more to it here.

Sam Hamill: Sometimes you write something and you think, "I got it." Then you come back to it a week later and you realize "this isn't really the end, this is a pause, but I have more to say in this way, and in this style and in this voice." If you're listening carefully to that voice you follow your voice. You have to bow to your muse.

Paul E Nelson: This gets to a question I had been meaning to ask you for a while and get on tape about the difference between the epic tradition, which we associate with Europe and America, and the serial tradition, which we associate more with a West Coast kind of sensibility, what Robin Blaser, and Robert Duncan and Jack Spicer talked about. Can you talk about the serial tradition and maybe how that's more of a West Coast thing than an East Coast or Midwest thing?

Sam Hamill: It seems to be more prominent among a certain group of West Coast poets. The poem in sequence can be inspired in various ways. One of them is simply through lyrical form, which provides a kind of syntax which one begins to follow and returns to that music, to that language with a certain ability to listen within yourself and extend that rhythm, extend that kind of speech, extend the meditation, but not in a narrative way, which is necessary of the epic. The epic has to have a narrative base. While there may be narrative impulses and shadows in the serial poem or the sequential poem, its root is not a narrative poem, its root is shorter and more lyrical.

Paul E Nelson: If there's a narrative thread it's often one that develops organically and maybe outside the awareness of the poet writing.

Sam Hamill: Yeah, yeah.

Paul E Nelson: "*Habitations*" has some of those elements of the serial poem, especially when we look at how you end with a phrase and then repeat with that phrase or something similar.

Sam Hamill: Well, I don't exactly repeat the phrase. I *inexactly* repeat the phrase, as Marvin Bell would say. You have to be careful about that sort of thing or it can become simply a device. Finding the measure, (Robert Kelly, has a wonderful poem by that title, "*Finding the Measure*") is finding the mantram, is finding how to proceed. It's inspirational. You have to listen to your muse. The more you force things syntactically, the further away you tend to get from the truth of the poem, as it were.

Paul E Nelson: When it's used as a device. Maybe you could speak a little bit to the dangers of that, or what that reflects, when something is being used as a device.

Sam Hamill: At issue is the matter of artifice. Artifice can make a poem and it can also destroy a poem. I think of that line from that wonderful George Seferis poem that I read last night, "We've loaded even our song with so much music that it's slowly sinking / and we've decorated our art so much that its features have been eaten away by gold." This idea that you can overload a work of art. You don't want to load up. Each of us has a slightly different impulse and it's being true to the impulse and being true to whatever your literary values, whatever your philosophical values are.

In my case, in the poem "Habitations" I was trying to connect in a very deep way with the ecology of the Northwest. In each of the poems there's a list of extinct animals, and plants and things. Thinking about those things that have gone extinct, except that they are still within us. They're within us within the imagination, but they're also biologically within us. It's organic poetry that's actually organic. (Laughter.)

Paul E Nelson: Well it's interesting, I'm reminded of the indigenous people who say that some scientists came and checked the genetics of a cedar tree and found salmon genes in it because the bears eat the salmon, the bears shit the salmon, and the salmon genes become part of that tree, literally part of that tree. That's what you're getting at.

What about the research to find these different extinct species? How did that happen?

Sam Hamill: That's abundantly available. There's plenty of information online, or in any library about animal, and plant and insect extinction. I had read a lot about it over the many years, so I didn't really have to look much up. I did look up a few things, but mostly the things I mention are things that I at one time or another studied. For instance, the Western Camel. When you think about camels roaming Puget Sound, it boggles the mind. There were camels here!

Paul E Nelson: Isn't that the fear of the average right-wing American, camels will return and we'll have to… (laughter.)

Sam Hamill: No, I think it's the camel herders that they worry about.

Paul E Nelson: The "camel jockeys." Right.

There are some great images, even just saying the names and hearing them aloud is rewarding. You talk about the phanopoeia, and there are just beautiful images that gallop across your mind's eye when you hear that poem.

Sam Hamill: There's also a kind of "Zen thusness" in that. There's a really wonderful Zen koan that says, "Why is the white horse not a horse?" It's way to pique the imagination and to try to engage the imagination and philosophy and history all at once.

Paul E Nelson: And an ethos.

Sam Hamill: Yeah and an ethos, of course.

Paul E Nelson: Of the human not being anthropocentric, but taking their rightful place in the great order of things.

Sam Hamill: Yes.

Paul E Nelson: To get back to that serial versus epic, I'm trying to get a sense of how the West Coast, and the Pacific Rim, for that matter, the Rexroth quote from the Morris Graves essay about how we on the West Coast owe more to Asian traditions then we do to European traditions. This notion of the serial poem as opposed to the epic I think is an important distinction.

With the epic we got the sense of the European and thus, the American, hero/white knight coming to the rescue, whether it's John Wayne, or the Knights of the Round Table, or whoever. We on the West Coast maybe don't buy into that as readily. Do you agree with that?

Sam Hamill: Well I think literarily no, but in terms of pop culture, we certainly do buy into it. In speaking of the literary community, I think there's a great deal of skepticism about that sort of thing. That skepticism really arose with people like Robinson Jeffers. Jeffers was the first West Coast poet. We owe a great deal to Jeffers, including his severe questioning of Western cultural traditions. That's sort of built into us as West Coast poets. Also, this is newer land than the East Coast, for we white invaders. We rub shoulders with Native Americans constantly whereas in New York City and Boston not so much.

Paul E Nelson: In front of the cigar store maybe. (Hamill laughs.)

Sam Hamill: We're open to that deeper sense of what we could biodiversity, both among human and non-human species. Linguistically, I would bet most white East Coast-type literary people their second language is French, not all of them, and there's some

Italian speakers, and German speakers and et cetera. But French is sort of the dominant literary language. It was French that really gave us our American poetry. The big influences on Pound and Williams and the people who came after Pound and Williams were French. You could say that American poetry has been hugely shaped by the French poets.

Paul E Nelson: Rimbaud, Mallarmé, people like that.

Sam Hamill: Sure. On the West Coast, beginning with people like Gary Snyder especially, but even before Snyder, you think of people like the Chinese translator, Witter Bynner. Guys like Witter Bynner. Those anthologies of Chinese poems had an enormous effect on American poetry across the board.

I once read an essay claiming that Pound's "Cathay" was the most influential book of the 20th century. It's just 14 poems, and 14 short poems by Li Po. Yet, it really brought that personal short lyric poem into American poetry. It didn't exist that way before.

On the West Coast, we had the beginnings of a Zen Buddhist practice in America and we had poets like Gary Snyder, Phil Whalen, and Kenneth Rexroth, who studied seriously ancient cultures and languages. That had a huge impact on all of us, much more than learning to speak French, for instance. If you're not a real student of Chinese or Japanese your chances are your second language is Spanish. There's a much bigger Spanish-speaking population that's not Puerto Rican. I don't mean to excuse Puerto Ricans from anything, it's just so many Puerto Ricans move to places like New York City that they created islands of basically Puerto Rican culture, which is fine, I'm not being critical. I'm just pointing out that in the West we had migrant workers, we had indigenous peoples, all of these things were there around us all the time and we were aware of them. It's really a difference sensibility between the West Coast and the East Coast.

Paul E Nelson: In fact, if you look at the Mission of San Juan Capistrano it goes back to 1776, which when you think about it, on the East Coast they were starting a country. On the West Coast, it was a Spanish colony at the time.

Jeffers was trained in the classics, spoke Latin and Greek, so in a way, he's this pinnacle of Western philosophy who came to the edge of the continent, said basically, "It dies here." That is basically his conclusion. Then he comes up with this notion of "inhumanism," which is sort of a crude attempt to suggest that we need to recognize our true place in the scheme of things.

Sam Hamill: It was his objection to living in an anthropocentric universe.

Paul E Nelson: Right. What are some other characteristics of a West Coast and Pacific Rim poetics?

Sam Hamill: Open space in our poems, poems about mountain ranges, poems about deserts, poems about prairies, poems about living among animals. These were the norm to us. The East Coast idea of nature is Thoreau, who on most nights walked for 20 minutes over to Emerson's house to get dinner while proclaiming his love of "nature" and saying that he could be happy living in an ammo box, which is absurd. It takes a Hayden Carruth 100 years later to point out to the absurdity of such an idea, whereas so many of us in the West, we grew up around cattle ranches and sheep ranches. There were mountains to climb, and places to wander. A lot of wandering in West Coast poetry.

On the other hand, it took a very long while for us to develop any kind of urban poetry at all. If you look at much of West Coast poetry where does our urban voice begin to rise? Well, maybe sometimes in Rexroth, maybe Roethke, I don't know. Whereas, the urban voices are constant in East Poetry. They have a different kind of richness. I'm not making this an either/or, I'm just pointing out a difference.

Paul E Nelson: It's the sense that this is a very young literary culture still.

Sam Hamill: Yeah. Oh yeah.

Paul E Nelson: In one way, it's a deficit because it's not mature. But in another way, it's here, ours, for the shaping.

Sam Hamill: In some ways, it's a deeply mature tradition because of our tendency to be more involved in what we would call deep ecology, or deep anthropology. When I was a child, for instance, understanding a little bit about Navajo and Hopi culture was just profound as all hell. That's something you wouldn't likely get going to school in Virginia. You might learn about the five civilized tribes, but you learn about them in a kind of remote way, whereas here I had friends who were Navajo and Hopi. Going to a sweat lodge for the first time, that's a kind of western/southwestern experience that's really bound up in a sense of place, and a sense of pre-American white male domination. You begin to see that on a real basis. It was one pointed out to me if you do a line a mile long, the last one inch of that line would cover all of the history of humanity. The beginning of that line is the beginning of planet Earth, so it tells you what a very tiny little bit of history we as human beings actually occupy.

Paul E Nelson: It's a flash.

Sam Hamill: When you look at it that way you can understand why someone like Pound or Rexroth would insist that genius is always contemporary and that Sophocles is as contemporary today as he ever was, you simply have to have eyes and ears to see and hear.

Paul E Nelson: The West Coast Beat Movement, interest in Buddhist culture, that's had an effect on the culture period, hasn't it?

Sam Hamill: Oh, of course it has. Without the Beat scene in the 50s there wouldn't have been any hippies. The hippies were just sort of the popularization of some aspects of the crazier edges of the Beat Movement. Anytime you have a movement, there's always a lunatic fringe. There were always more movement followers than movement makers. Followers are, whatever else they are, followers. Rexroth, Duncan, Snyder, et cetera, they created a spark that started a fire, part of which burned out of control.

If you look at the Beat writers there were all of these fringe people. There were really only five or six of them who were actually really remarkable writers. There were then all of these sort of fringe types who became a cliché, women wearing black leotards and hanging out late at night in smoky jazz clubs, and the romance of all of that.

Paul E Nelson: And the guy with the beret, and the bongos-

Sam Hamill: Sure, sure.

Paul E Nelson: The Maynard G. Krebs kind of cliché.

Sam Hamill: Sure, curiously studious hipness. Being hip. You simply had to be hip. That was essential. That's largely a waste of time, being hip. (Laughter.)

Paul E Nelson: You're hip, aren't you?

Sam Hamill: I was very hip. I wasn't just hip, I was cool. (Laughs.)

Paul E Nelson: Which begs the question that Tower of Power asked, "What is hip?"
The poem Eyes Wide Open… You mentioned the story about the American Friends Service Committee and an exhibit of thousands of pairs of empty boots suggesting this is part of the loss of the Iraq War. You've got a quote in there, "Empty saddles in the old corral, where do they ride tonight?" The line before that says, "When I was a child frightened of the night and crying in my bed my father told me a poem, or sang." Can you tell a little bit about that story?

Sam Hamill: (Singing.) Empty saddles in the old corral, where do they ride tonight?

Paul E Nelson: You didn't sing it last night!

Sam Hamill: It was a 1930s cowboy song, sloppy, silly romantic, but kind of charming in a hokey way. Of course, when you're a kid, wow. I grew up on a horse.

(Flicking cigarette ashes, Hamill makes an aside: "We'll use my Buddhist baking bowl for an ashtray.")

I grew up in a cowboy culture and I apparently was a pretty badly abused infant. I had the night terrors. Going to bed was a really scary time for me because I didn't know whether I was going to have nightmares or whether I would actually sleep. Him reciting poems, or reading poems, or singing some of these cowboy songs would really calm me down. I'd have him sing it again and the second time through I'd start falling asleep. Maybe the third time through I would drift off into sleep.

Paul E Nelson: This was your adopted family?

Sam Hamill: Yeah.

Paul E Nelson: This is in Utah?

Sam Hamill: Yeah.

Paul E Nelson: Born in Northern California, but raised in Utah until you left at about age what, 13, 14?

Sam Hamill: 14.

Paul E Nelson: 14 years old. left from there to go to San Francisco?

Sam Hamill: Yeah, yeah. I got busted in Reno, sent back, stayed a couple of months, ran away again at 15 and that was when I pretty much stayed away until I went back and tried to spend a little bit of time in high school, because Kenneth [Rexroth] had convinced me that you got to have an education. However you're going to get it you got to get it. I was doing some pretty bad shit on the streets in San Francisco, so I went back to take a shot at high school. You could imagine trying to go to a high school in Holladay, Utah after having spent most of a year hanging out with people like Kenneth Rexroth, so that wasn't working out. I knew I needed some discipline, so I enlisted in the Marine Corps for a ticket out of there.

Paul E Nelson: At 17.

Sam Hamill: Yeah.

Paul E Nelson: Don't give them any ideas. [Lowering enlistment age.] We might start that program up again.

On page 17 of *Measured by Stone*, you said, "the 'struggle for poetry' in the world cannot take place in a museum." That phrase is in quotes, the "struggle for poetry."

Sam Hamill: (Lights a cigarette.) There are poets that produce what I call a museum of ideas. I'm not going to name names because that's sort of pointless, it's distracting. What I'm talking about is the idea of being alive in a living language and trying to find the truth of the essential experience of this, or that, or the other, being receptive to the change that is constant within all of us. My theory about fixed forms is that they tend to invite people to think in fixed ideas, which is why you have so many fixed meters. Whereas, in actual life it doesn't come at you that way, it's in bits, and pieces, and starts, and jumps and leaps, sometimes flowing very smoothly like a river, sometimes blowing apart like a tire. This museum of ideas is like, for instance, romantic poetry. To most of us these days an actual romantic poem sounds pretty bad, it's got end rhyme, it's probably in pentameter, and you're talking about your emotions rather than actually having any emotions or actually stirring any emotions.

For me though, the function of the poem is to tell its tale, but to do it with an emotional base that is felt as well as reasoned.

Paul E Nelson: Zukofsky's quote comes to mind and he said, "Only emotion objectified endures."

Sam Hamill: Well, yeah.

Paul E Nelson: The next thing is on that same page, in that same poem, we're talking about the poem "Arguing with Milosz in Vilnius." You say here, "The poem, a record of survival." Why don't you flesh that out a little bit.

Sam Hamill: Well, in the context of Milosz of course, he's a World War II exile who took up a home in France from which he basically exiled himself to the United States. I'm an orphan, that makes me a permanent exile. I'm an atheist in a basically religious country, another kind of exile, philosophical exile, existentialism. Simply being a poet in a culture like this creates a kind of exile because we're uncommon, we're very uncommon people with uncommon likes, and dislikes and passions. It's not a big stretch.

Paul E Nelson: The poem written by you or someone like you as a record of survival. This is the daily task of trying to exist in a culture that doesn't appreciate poems.

Sam Hamill: Well trying to live reasonably in an irrational culture.

Paul E Nelson: You say that being a poet in this culture is rare, but yet, we've had in the last 20 years an explosion of MFA programs, and creative writing programs, and as a result, an explosion of poets. You said last night, "Everybody's a poet and everybody's an editor." (Laughter.)

Sam Hamill: Well in a way that's true. I think that's altogether basically a good thing. We've created a kind of target audience for poetry and I think that's a little bit dangerous. We've also created a kind of business class of poets. I think this is what people really object to when they badmouth the MFA programs the way it gets to turn into a little corner of academia. It would be much better for our culture if a lot of those people would get out of academia and come and live in the real world, as it were. It would be nice if I wasn't the only regularly publishing poet in Anacortes, which I guess I am, I don't know of another one. I know there are people who write poetry, you can find them among the 30,000 poems in "Poets Against War." It's the way there are millions of painters as well, but how many really serious painters are there at any given point. There were quite a few, but they're not in the thousands, maybe in the hundreds.

Paul E Nelson: The danger in this business class category for poets is that they run the risk of creating this kind of elitism that's separate from people?

Sam Hamill: Well, I'm not opposed to elitism. People use that word in the pejorative. I just think I spent a lot of years trying to get a grip on classical Chinese and Japanese poetry and philosophy. The people who have translated that stuff with any of degree of success, that's a very small club. I'm happy to be a member of that club.

Paul E Nelson: What is the danger then of the business class of poets, the MFA graduates?

Sam Hamill: What happens is people with a problem with their ego build little cliques, and turfs and neighborhoods, and they become the little lords of their little neighborhood. A little humility before the task is a good idea. When you build followers, you don't build leaders. Followers aren't leaders. Poets need to be leaders of their language and leaders of their art.

Paul E Nelson: It's very interesting that the next question I had planned, had to do with the section of your book that's entitled, "Lessons From Thieves." I don't need to make such an intentional segue, but that's where I was going before you went into that last bit about the ego—the building of the business class of poets, to use your words. Maybe you can read the last thread about the business class as standing in opposition to that Confucian basic teaching. If we go back to the Confucius quote and the way you explained it on the ferry—

Sam Hamill: The great learning.

Paul E Nelson: In the great learning we see where this business class begins to be part of the danger of that by building the ego.

Sam Hamill: Well the neo-Confucians were a perfect example of how you corrupt the fundamentally wonderful teachings of Confucius. You create an enormous bureaucracy within which everyone is struggling for their own turf. The same thing happens in the poetry community when you get into the business of it, who gets the paycheck, who gets to give the reading, who gets to be the master teacher. People who are master teachers for a livelihood and who do this constantly, what a weird perspective on the world! Day in and day out, you're talking to this little handful of people who are your admirers. It's difficult, I would think, for someone like that to keep their head above the water.

Paul E Nelson: Where you have acolytes.

Sam Hamill: Yeah.

Paul E Nelson: Yeah, yeah, yeah.

Sam Hamill: And sycophants.

Paul E Nelson: Sycophants, yeah. There's a line in *Testament of the Thief*, "I never cause a disturbance, no too loud laughter, no angry glance." Is there an anecdote that goes with that "no too loud laughter"?

Sam Hamill: One of the knocks on me is I'm too intense. I have a very famous, very loud laugh. I've been criticized for that by certain kinds of people, so I'm just thumbing my nose at them.

Paul E Nelson: My neighbor at the new SPLAB said, "I knew things were going well because I could hear your laugh through the walls." I'm thinking okay, no too loud laughter, very good. I'm not in the thief category when it comes to that… But the ability to have that kind of laugh is what you're getting at, the ability to be so open and vulnerable that you can have that kind of laugh.

Sam Hamill: Well, and in my case, I'm deaf and that makes a lot of me loud. We deaf people we don't know how loud our voice is, we really can't tell. We tend to be loud because we don't hear ourselves. But I was loud before I was deaf. I'm just kind of a boisterous kind of guy sometimes. Sometimes I'm very quiet.

Paul E Nelson: And your intensity?

Sam Hamill: Well, what about it? (Laughter.)

Paul E Nelson: Where do you think that comes from and why is it so feared in this culture?

Sam Hamill: Well, first of all, I paid certain kinds of prices for the way I've conducted my life. I spent many years in a kind of voluntary poverty. I was nearly 20 years at Copper Canyon Press before I started getting a paycheck. I taught in prisons and I learned to really love those men. Even though some of them did really horrible things I saw how the system screws them over. Yet, as I used to tell my students there, they can keep you behind bars, but they can't imprison your imagination. Your imagination is where you really live anyway, whether you're in jail or not. It's really about what you do with your imagination. I have an idea about spending my life in the service of something larger than myself, or something larger than the consumption of goods. That was to be in the service of poetry. A lot of people don't understand what that entails. They see my attitude and my frankness as threatening. But that, frankly, is more their problem than my problem. I'm not a threat to anyone. I'm devoted to non-violence, but I'm also devoted to appreciating a non-materialist culture and to creating a non-materialist culture. I'm a socialist who lives in a capitalist state, which means that I'm confronted every day by the profound immoralism of my own country.

Paul E Nelson: And a culture which fears someone like you who dedicates their life to something non-material.

Sam Hamill: It's repressive.

Paul E Nelson: That goes to the core of how you left Copper Canyon Press.

Sam Hamill: Yeah, yeah.

Paul E Nelson: Something wrong with a culture that allows something like that to happen.

Sam Hamill: Well of course there is, but it happens all the time. What they did to me was what George Bush did to Iraq. They build up a straw man, and say he's threatening and let's get him.

Paul E Nelson: Right.

Sam Hamill: Saddam, you know?

Paul E Nelson: The people who listen to this in retrospect who are all hoping that the election of November 2, 2010 didn't turn out the way it's likely to turn out, they wonder what happens to these guys who set up the straw men? Where is the justice? Can we take solace in the fact that anytime there's hubris involved the person's going to go down or is there more to it than that?

Sam Hamill: No, there's no reason why we should expect justice in a system that's built the way our system is built. As long as they're going to engage in the politics of personal destruction, as Carl Rove called it, then anything is fair game; rumor, innuendo, blasphemy, lies, deceits, double dealings, it's all business and American business people do this all the damn time.

Paul E Nelson: If you've got money you can do it.

Sam Hamill: Yeah, sure.

Paul E Nelson: That justifies it.

Sam Hamill: Sure.

Paul E Nelson: Bill Ransom said a very interesting thing. I told him about my situation in Auburn. You look at a typical South or Central American country and there's a coup d'etat and what's the first thing that happens? First they take over the radio station, then they shoot the poets. What am I doing in Auburn? I'm doing radio and poetry. Bill said, "But in this country they don't assassinate you, they assassinate your character."

Sam Hamill: Yeah, oh yeah. Yeah, spot on.

Paul E Nelson: Page 47, the iletta "The 'Nine Gates Series'." It's a really beautiful poem. You didn't read that last night.

Sam Hamill: First of all, it's nine poems long. Each one of those poems is a meditation and should be meditated on.

Paul E Nelson: It would be nice to hear it read sometime.
Anyway, the last bit of number eight I guess it is, yeah, is "a guy standing by me at a Levertov reading 20 years ago whispers in my ear, 'She reads just like she talks, except her voice seems to come from somewhere else'." It's a great anecdote. To me, it also goes to what she and Robert Duncan were talking about in the early '60s in their correspondence about organic poetry, and that goes to Robin Blaser's essay "The Practice of Outside," this notion that the source of the poem is outside of us. Even if it's in a trust of the language to go

where it needs to go, there is this kind of sublimation to something bigger, in this case, the process, and with her, not just with the writing, but with the actual reading of it in public.

Sam Hamill: Oh yeah, yeah, sure.

Paul E Nelson: Tell us about it.

Sam Hamill: All of us who are real poets, when we read the poem there's a different quality in the voice even though the tone of the voice and the words are the same tone and words. It's what the poetry itself does with the voice. It's the music of the mind moving among the 10,000 things.
From this same sequence…

[Hamill reads from the poem Nine Gates, Part 5.]

Before poetry
was called poetry, what was
its name? Before truth
was a word, there was still truth
and it had a name. Shih-shuang,

writing long ago,
thought words were "expedient
means." Buddhas are born
of necessity. Shih-shuang
himself must have groped along.

Words are expedient means, but they're not the result, they're not a consequence, they're not an arrival. They're a means.

Paul E Nelson: An approximation.

Sam Hamill: And words evolve and change, and meanings change. A poem is, in its own way, a provisional conclusion.

Paul E Nelson: Provisional. It's the best you can achieve in the moment.

Sam Hamill: Yeah.

Paul E Nelson: When the history of West Coast or Pacific Rim poetics is written, how does Denise Levertov fit in?

Sam Hamill: Elusively. First of all, she's not a West Coaster. I once criticized her for too many inversions in a poem. She laughed and me and she said, "You just don't understand, I have a Mid-Atlantic accent." She was born and raised in England, and came to America and spent most of her life living in Boston, and Maine and New York, and then moved late in her life to Seattle. Her poetics, as her huge correspondence Robert Duncan makes abundantly clear, is primary philosophical material for West Coast poetry. She was a projective verse poet, an organic poet. Her essays on organic poetry, both of which are absolutely wonderful.

Paul E Nelson: *Some Notes on Organic Form*?

Sam Hamill: Yeah.

Paul E Nelson: And, *The Function of The Line.* Those two specifically?

Sam Hamill: Yeah, yeah.

Paul E Nelson: You've already done your spiel on line breaks, so people can probably refer to that because you've done it enough. Too many poets are writing mediocre prose broken up into line breaks. If you can have that clever kind of end that's their notion, the typical notion, of line breaks, but it's a lot deeper than that.

Sam Hamill: One of the dangers of work-shopping is that you learn to rely on things like wit. If you can make something witty, you

get a kind of immediate response. But it's *only* immediate and in a
way it's a kind of low-grade response, it's kind of a cheap response. I
said of the "Nine Gates" that they were meditations and they needed
to be meditated on and that's why I didn't read them. I mean that in
a very serious way.

Workshops tend to produce "Group-Think" and we tend to
start writing like one another because we're getting together twice
a week or once a week, and spending hours going over our poems.
There's some good in that back and forth-ness of it, but there's
also this risk of Group-Think and of relying simply on a poetry of
wit, and not thinking carefully about the process of being a poetry.
That is, how do you find and follow what's given. Poetry is, after all,
above all else, a gift. It's a gift to the poet from the muse, that thing
we call inspiration, which the poet and the act of being a poet, a
maker, transforms in order to give it away so that someone can hear
the poem, read the poem, feel the poem and want to respond to
that poem by saying, "Oh, I can't wait to give this away." It really is
a condition of gift economics. But it's a gift that also comes with a
certain responsibility.

If your primary goal is to be popular, workshops are a really
good thing because you find out what works in the workshop. If
your design is not simply to be popular, but to really, deeply engage
a tradition, then that workshop is a distraction more than anything
else because it's drawing you away from the tradition that you should
be excavating, like an archeologist. You should be studying these
stones instead of wetting your finger and seeing which way the wind
blows.

Paul E Nelson: Like Olson calling one of his books "Archeologist
of Morning."

Sam Hamill: Yeah. Well as you know, he was a very good amateur
archeologist.

Paul E Nelson: Yeah, him digging into the Mayan culture was part
of that.

When we get into that Group-Think we're also conditioning ourselves not to recognize the peculiar gifts that the muse has for us as individuals and unable to really achieve our deepest gesture as an individual in that way, that's part of what you're saying, right?

Sam Hamill: Yeah, yeah.

Paul E Nelson: What is it exactly? If you can make it literal. You've told me this before, the sound of the-

Sam Hamill: Well poetry is a temple of words, a temple made of words. Poetry.

Paul E Nelson: The literal translation in English has to do with the hand reaching down cradling a seedling, so how does that...

Sam Hamill: Well there's a hook on the bottom of this character. What that hook represents is the hand reaching down with the seedling in it that is about to plant the seed. Poetry is where seeds get planted, or poetry is a planting of seeds, you might say. But you can also say that poetry is a temple. That's the wonderful thing about Chinese entomology, you can get hooked on this shit like Ezra Pound did and get completely off track, but that particular character I think is quite wonderful, the character for word combined with the character for temple to get poetry.

Paul E Nelson: Well one last main subject here, one of the later poems in the book "Poem on His sixty-third Birthday," second stanza, "I did not choose to be born/ in springtime, the briefest season, / but I may choose the day I die/ if reason dictates such a choice be made/ any a day like this one would suffice." Which goes back to the saying that we associate with Native American warriors, "Today is a good day to die." Is that you proclaiming your warrior nature, also proclaiming your rights as a person who says, "Look, I'm going to do a Kevorkian thing if I have to?"

Sam Hamill: That latter. I'm not a warrior. I find that the warrior language, warrior culture really bothers me a lot.

Paul E Nelson: Even the spiritual warrior?

Sam Hamill: You can't be a spiritual warrior, you can't. Being a warrior is antithetical to spiritualism.

Paul E Nelson: Why?

Sam Hamill: Because warrior implies aggression and spiritualism requires acceptance.

Paul E Nelson: You talked about the koan, the "sound of one hand" as opposed to the "sound of one hand clapping." There was a moment where that student was ready to disembowel himself until he got it. Could that person be seen as a spiritual warrior?

Sam Hamill: No, that was Hakuin. Buddhism has to begin with an idea about not killing. Now you can't not kill, you have to eat. For you to eat, something must die. A lot of people, for instance say, "I don't eat things that have faces" that's their way of dealing with it. That's not a warrior spirit. It's antithetical, as I was saying. But I would also point out that the monastic life is not something that I've ever experienced or ever wanted to experience. As close as I ever got to that was the U.S. Marine Corps, which is a warrior culture. (Laughs.)

Paul E Nelson: Well, I'm glad we got this final part down, Sam. Thanks for your generosity of spirit.

Sam Hamill: A pleasure.

Old Friend
(For Sam Hamill, after Li Po)

We wander through asphalt riparian zones
until it hits each of us: it IS later than we thought.

Another quick trip between this veil of soul-making
and complete re-calibration to the ultimate mystery.

The Moon-Rabbit's elixir we learn was a metaphor
but the message could have come from a House Finch.

Dead, they ready our friend's bones for the last fire
and if we're paying attention, we get ready
      for the next grief wave.

He warned us this life was mist and he,
for one, did not fear the hereafter.

His Zen studies readied him for the notion
      of anything after here
      as one more illusion.

Paul E Nelson
7:53am – 4.15.2018

Letter to Sam Hamill

Dear Sam,

        When I search the past for you
       you'd not be Basho sleeping
          next to pissing horses, or
Li Bai dead drunk reaching for
  the full moon's reflection. (You
     can rarely see the Cascadia
      moon & you're more a sea guy
than a man about rivers.
    Leave that for Sund and the cult.)
        More measured than falling for
  that old reflection trick, though
his moon lunge might've been the
      equivalent of Kevorkian
     in T'ang era Xi'an. And
      the boots remain muddy. How
Rexroth's alive inside you.
     The last first guy here looking east.

    I think about how you love
      to tell stories and I'm always
      happy to set you up. Take
  Long Tall Dexter at Centrum.
They're gonna play scales even
if they're the "Master Class." (How
  THAT phrase reverberates
  w/ the unwillingness to
  humble one's self. Ah Port
  Townsend! Will you visit there
  after your last taste of cold
  Otokoyama, return
     as a whisper in the poplars
of Cape George, or leading the

Congress of Trees? We're still
  digesting your last will and
    testimony, your final
  Habitation.

I thought it was your "Zen golf
  concentration" w/ which you
    screened out backswing distractions
  but no, just yr hearing aid
    turned off. How, at Avalon
      you'll watch the eagles, know a
        baby eagle as it flies
  overhead while you shoot for
          birdies after a good drive,
or settle for a lay up &
      take your bogie like a man.

        Nowadays four thousand face
                book friends'll keep your keyboard
    chattering about fracking,
    Guantanamo, bigot's parades,
    modern day McCarthy's,
outsized CEO's pay or
            Rachel Corrie mixed in w/
a dash of the masters, strive
    to be a poet of modest
        renown taking Kuan Yin over
            Christ for Christ's sake. Happy
    w/ cold Momokawa.

How you'd say in an interview
you cd do the Kevorkian
          (not in so many words) your
    last poems of the melancholic
          but if generosity be love,
your love studies paid back abundant.

& they're'll be stories galore
maybe the zen bootcamp you ran
                    called a Writer's Workshop
               & continued resentment
                    from the "dilettante periphery"
        you'd warn about over &
                         over having felt their wrath
        they who'd envy you, want a
foto w/ you but not want
        the 5A wakeups and strange
              languages, or how they'd court
                    the company of dabblers to
approximate the feelings
         of masters, the life-long shortcuts
                    you refused to take.
              In death, you'll be a wise-ass
        Raven above the ferns &
               moss, urging a poet yet-
               to-be w/ a perfect seven
        beat image, then gone — a blur
                of black in one of a *hundred*
                    avenues of gray across the sky
                    as we hunker down for life
                    without that irascible
        orphan who lived it all as
              a sacramental relationship
that lasts always always urging us
        to live as if we'll be *measured*
by stone.

With Love and Gratitude,

Paul Nelson
12:13p — 3.15.14
After Kenneth Rexroth

A Simple Gift
for Sam Hamill

Yes, dear and oldest friend, every fall
the wounded saguaro fill with rain
from the Gulf of Mexico,
their priestly shadows suffer blizzards
that tore through the bad old days, years
the highway conjured a simpler horizon.
Remember how the bald tires
blew? Not in the whitest heat of Zion
summer, but in our unlikely return—
rain drumming Me and Bobby McGhee
against the windshield, singing Creeley
from the Great Salt Lake to the distant sea.
Perhaps it's true, where coyote groans
in the poisoned canyon, a drifting road
calls our bones. Clouds tumble, a paycheck
arrives, we set out for other mountains,
under cold beasts orphaned by Orion.

Dawn rolls across the desert, over us
camped beside the unknowing flowing—
the beautiful Williams River. We boil old
grounds over a twiggy fire and drive all day
with the river's breath and pulse—to reclaim
ways of seeing long since lost. Broken down,
the valves smoking miles shy of Eureka,
we wait beside the highway for help
or the law and at dusk share the last can
of Chef-Boy-Ar-Dee. Maybe it's true,
we've had enough blistering sun,
perched in this imaginary mecca
that neither forgives nor grieves.

Friend, even in the early days
we knew the poets who blazed trails
and fought exile would be freed only by
death. McGrath has left the old high road
for hieroglyphic fire, Kenneth's temple bell
no longer rings in the ears of swallows.
Art Blakey's metalflake snares dance
only in the heart's garden. The garden's
heart longs to break in sixteenth notes
Coltrane used to blow to reach his heaven,
a real gone, deep-fired perfection.
And the day! See how it frees itself
from the light, how it bears us in its belly,
in an insignificant meal of muffins
and eggs, in the solitary life built
of renga, thick cedar, buddha dog
and his shameless nature. An egg
cradled in the hand remains an egg,
whether a dying chick or yolk that blooms—
it's the prayer sung by a deaf mute,
the fear retold by the generations,
the indifference of the ocean
that balances the inner ear.

The road rolls out before us,
past the beet packing plant
and the dry beds of Utah,
to places we have never been.
Let us go, in this single cyclic gift
that cannot be withheld: our song.

William O'Daly

[Originally published in *Susurrus*, Guest Writer, Spring 2011]

Habitation

a letter for Sam Hamill

Sam, I've been living
in *Habitation*, your book
of living poems,
and I'm struck like a bell how
completely you've lived your vow.

You have made a life
in service to a temple
not of money or
of power or worse yet of
prestige but of words spoken

simply, having come
to that grace, so that they mean
exactly what they
say. You have been a monk and
fool because we have to be

fools to keep thriving
in this world with its deadly
imitations, words
abused everywhere to mean
nothing, which is everything

when everything is
meant to be sold. As the things
of the marketplace
circulate among thieves, you've
given away treasures, songs

for all seasons sung
in true measures, showing us
one way to open
our hearts, free for a moment
of self and of suffering.

All that disturbs us
you once wrote in a poem
can be felt, absorbed,
and finally transcended
by the act of listening

to that deepest voice
speaking from within. That's why
you have found the right
name for your book, this record
of your life and your habit

of deep listening,
which has been your monk's robes, your
practice and precept,
your way of perception that
makes it all new, and makes you

all new, no longer
a creature but creator
of habit, living
the epiphany we find
in the poem wherein all

is music, is light.

Thomas H. Pruiksma

The Calling

~ For the poet Sam Hamill (5.9.43-4.14.18)

What do I say to a man who loved me once?
Once fierce
broken wreckage
wrenched from marrow
love. I'd forgotten

his letters to me typed, the letter A double tapped
buried in my basement shoved
in a box I'd forgotten
bitter mildew
sleeved papers.

On the envelopes, postage
13¢. I'd forgotten

*Your poem is fine but you should not say "evergreen." Not a dog,
a black dog, not a black dog, a Lab. No "grow like an evergreen"
but "I grow ever green as spruce or fir." "Yas yas yas."*

*Write from the blood. Just write
and write.* Why these letters
I'd forgotten
today while he lay dying? Why?

From one envelope, his poem.
I unfold his voice
Turning again to the sea, the immense
And female sea ...
What
have I come to? I have felt tides
urging at my loins, the *pale wings of the moon...*
The sea and psyche flame, burn
I kneel, kissing
the smoke. I'd forgotten

to write him back
to write at all. Forgotten
this bruising, swollen love
how *the salt of blood thickens my tongue.*
O to find him to tell him
yas yas yas *across the calling*
of forever I am alive.

Heidi Seaborn

A Pair of Hanging Scrolls: *Landscape and Couplet of Chinese Verse* (late 18th century) by Ike Taiga

for Sam Hamill

I'm not thinking of the mulberry tree, its *abrazos*
white with flowers, its branches emerging from its gnarled
trunk that fall back toward the earth, or how the spring snow
matched its delicacy, before it melted into the new grass,
and left the tree standing in the snow of its own fallen
blossoms, but of you, Sam. How persistent… trunk scarred
with many other seasons, the new sapling sprouting
upward, as some spire of green to heaven,
emerges from its base, while its bark
thickens and sheds. Not even the mulberry tree
can hold your passing …so the mind wheels
among metaphors of lodestone and north star,
your presence to which I turned so often. Oh,
now a spiraling movement, unfixed, the night sky wheels
into morning – the pot of coffee on the stove, the boiling
water I pour into my love's cup. When they said you
had left, I left the brightly lit screen
in the brightly lit house and went out into
the dark to stand and, silently, bow, to you, and heaven –
that clear light of the void. For the word is not only
what persists, but what the word resists.

You knew we are not so much "lost in nature,"
as nature is lost in us. Our cultivation of mental
construction that tries to capture while it evades. Oh,
divine tree where the three-legged Sun Bird
was said to reside, linking earth to eastern heaven,
budding only when the risk of frost is past, thus
cultivating patience, its flesh made into paper, strips
hung in branches as prayers, pulped to be made
into vessels for a Shinto shrine, hanging scrolls

or this byōbu —luminous Shrine of the Water God
where waterfalls forever fall. Even its leaves
fed to those silkworms that spun the fabrics worn by
the samurai and the ruling class, thus becoming
a symbol of nurturing, self-sacrifice, a kind of weapon
deployed by human persistence, the first bow
made by the Emperor Huangdi to kill the tiger
that had treed him in a mulberry tree, and among
all this, a single pilgrim: "The man...likely
to be the poet himself," climbing a "towering
mountain of an almost impossible steepness."

No, I cannot give you the mulberry tree, even if
I change its arabesques to *abrazos*. It is itself,
as you were, singular, alone. Whatever it was
that made me stop and bow toward the silence,
that moment – standing in the Metropolitan
and looking at Taiga's panel painting from the Edo
period, but not seeing the image at all, seeing
only your name on the attending note, as if you stood
there before me in your translation of Li Po, that one
I published years ago, when you were just crossing
the yellow river, transfixed *until*
only the mountain remained. What remains –
late in the afternoon, passing under the mulberry tree,
bent low because its branches scrape my bowing head,
an angle of declining light revealing the bark torqued
by sinews of strength coursing through its trunk – *is.*
How it eludes us – the nature of things resisting the nets
the mind casts out to harvest meaning from the air.
Oh fear and desire that makes of all it meets
a wrathful or a beautiful god. What persists is what
resists – flying fearlessly and without desire
into the clear light of the void.

Rebecca Seiferle

Nine Bows for a Brother Monk
For Sam Hamill (1943-April 14, 2018)

Just heard the news a couple hours ago, Sam.
Went out to buy a bottle of junmai ginjo sake
to celebrate, set a cup for you on the bookcase
by a copy of your Habitation and a begging bowl,
bowed nine times in your direction, filled our cups
and drank them both. Kanpai! Filled them again,
and again. And now, half drunk, I write these lines
in your honor, my brother monk, beloved immortal.

Karma Tenzing Wangchuk

Sam Hamill, Alexis Bernaut, Juliette Combes Latour and Cate Gable

At Shakespeare & Company, Paris: Shakespeare and Co (from left):
Gaëlle Prigent, Isabelle Lagny, John Mitchell, Alexis Bernaut,
Kaaren Kitchell, Sam Hamill, Delia Morris, Salal Al Hamdani,
Rosalind (Last name unknown.)

Biographies

Alexis Bernaut

Poet, translator, and musician Alexis Bernaut was born in Paris, France, in 1977. He published Au *matin suspendu* (Suspended in The Morning) in December 2012. In 2016, he was invited to the Seoul International Writers Festival. Some of his poems have been translated into English, Korean, and Hebrew. He met Sam Hamill in Paris in May 2014, through their mutual friend, French-Iraqi poet Salah Al Hamdani. Along with Delia Morris, Dominique Delpirou, and André Ughetto, he translated and published the first - and so far only - collection of Sam Hamill's poetry in France (*Ce que l'eau sait, Le Temps des Cerises*, 2016). He also translated into French Sam's version of the Wen fu. Alexis currently lives in Brittany, Western France, with his partner Gaelle, cats, horses, and donkeys.

Ian Boyden

Ian Boyden—artist, writer, translator, and curator—investigates relationships between the self and the environment, in particular how art and writing can shape our ecology. Consistent across his productions are his interests in material relevance and place-based thought, as well as a deep awareness of East Asian philosophies and aesthetics. He studied for many years in China and Japan, and holds degrees in the History of Art from Wesleyan University and Yale University. In addition to his independent projects, he also collaborates with scientists, poets, composers, and visual artists. He has exhibited widely, including a solo exhibition in China at the I.M Pei-designed Suzhou Museum. His books, paintings, and sculptures are found in many public collections including Reed College, Stanford University, the Portland Art Museum, and the Victoria & Albert Museum.

Leszek Chudziński

Leszek Chudziński has published poems in Poland (Attempt of Imagination: Almanac of Young Poetry, Poznań), in Japan (Kobe Haiku), in the U.S. and Canada, both in Polish and English. His poetry appeared in The Schuylkill Valley Journal (Philadelphia), Polish News (Chicago), FrogPond (Toronto), Strumien (Vancouver, BC), Lithuanus (Chicago), in an anthology of Polish-Canadian and Polish-American Poets, Wiatry (The Winds, Vancouver, BC). Most recently he pubished a bilingual (Polish-English) book of poetry, Sunday Poets, Miniatura, Krakow 2018, translated into English with Lyn Coffin.

Lyn Coffin

Lyn Coffin has had more than 30 of her books (poetry, fiction, drama, non-fiction, translations) published by W.W. Norton, Ithaca House Press and others. Her poems have been translated into six languages. William Meredith awarded Lyn's translations of the Czech poet Jiri Orten first prize in International Review's translation competition. Joyce Carol Oates included Lyn's story in Best American Short Stories ... and she was praised by Sam for her editing of Habitation. www.lyncoffin.com

Michael Daley

Michael Daley is a retired Mount Vernon High School teacher. His work has appeared in Ploughshares, Hudson Review, Rhino, Seattle Review, APR, and elsewhere. His fifth collection of poetry, True Heresies, is forthcoming from Cervena Barva Press in 2019. He lives near Deception Pass in Washington.

Martín Espada

Martín Espada was born in Brooklyn, New York in 1957. He has published almost twenty books as a poet, editor, essayist and translator. His latest collection of poems from Norton is called *Vivas to Those Who Have Failed* (2016). Other books of poems include: *The Trouble Ball* (2011), *The Republic of Poetry* (2006), *Alabanza* (2003), *A Mayan Astronomer in Hell's Kitchen* (2000), *Imagine the Angels of Bread* (1996),

City of Coughing and Dead Radiators (1993) and *Rebellion is the Circle of a Lover's Hands* (1990). His many honors include the 2018 Ruth Lilly Poetry Prize, the Shelley Memorial Award, the Robert Creeley Award, the National Hispanic Cultural Center Literary Award, an American Book Award, an Academy of American Poets Fellowship, the PEN/Revson Fellowship and a Guggenheim Fellowship. *The Republic of Poetry* was a finalist for the Pulitzer Prize. The title poem of his collection *Alabanza*, about 9/11, has been widely anthologized and performed. His book of essays, *Zapata's Disciple* (1998), was banned in Tucson as part of the Mexican-American Studies Program outlawed by the state of Arizona, and has been issued in a new edition by Northwestern University Press. A former tenant lawyer in Greater Boston's Latino community, Espada is a professor of English at the University of Massachusetts-Amherst.

Cate Gable

Cate Gable has a poetry MFA from Pacific Lutheran University; an MA from the University of WA; and a BA from University of Pennsylvania. Gable won first place in a San Francisco Bay Guardian poetry contest; an honorable mention in the 2019 Hoffman Center for the Arts Manzanita Poetry Contest; and an award-winning chapbook, *Heart* (Center for Creative Work). Most recently, she authored a book of poetry and commentary on Stein/Toklas, entitled *Chere Alice: Three Lives* (Publications Studio, Portland, OR.) and her poem "Kilauea" was selected for Hawaii Public Radio Aloha Shorts. Gable writes a weekly column for *The Chinook Observer*. She lives in Nahcotta, Washington and Paris, France.

Kim Goldberg

Kim Goldberg is the author of 8 books of poetry and nonfiction, Her *Devolution* collection of poems will be published by Caitlin Press in 2020. She lives in Nanaimo, BC.

Shaun Griffin

Shaun T. Griffin co-founded and directed Community Chest, a rural social justice agency for twenty-seven years. *Because the Light*

Will Not Forgive Me–Essays from a Poet, is forthcoming from the University of Nevada Press in 2019. Southern Utah University Press released *Anthem for a Burnished Land*, a memoir, in 2016. He edited *From Sorrow's Well–The Poetry of Hayden Carruth*, published by the University of Michigan Press in 2013. *This Is What the Desert Surrenders, New and Selected Poems*, came out from Black Rock Press in 2012. For over three decades, he and his wife Debby have lived in Virginia City.

Marilyn Hacker

Marilyn Hacker is the author of fourteen books of poems, including *Blazons* (Carcanet 2019), *A Stranger's Mirror* (Norton, 2015) and *Names* (Norton, 2010), and an essay collection, *Unauthorized Voices* (Michigan, 2010). Her sixteen translations of French and Francophone poets include Vénus Khoury-Ghata's *A Handful of Blue Earth* (Liverpool, 2017) and Emmanuel Moses' *Preludes and Fugues* (Oberlin, 2016). She lives in Paris.

José Kozer

José Kozer, born La Habana, 1940. Has Lived in the USA since 1960. Taught at Queens College (CUNY) from 1965 to 1997 and then retired in Hallandale, Florida. He is the author of some one hundred books of poetry, a couple of prose, has been translated into many languages and studied extensively in dissertations in U.S. universities. In 2013 he received the Pablo Neruda Award from the Chilean government and in 2017 became a Montgomery Fellow.

Stephen Kuusisto

Stephen Kuusisto directs The Burton Blatt Institute's Interdisciplinary Programs in disability at Syracuse University where he holds a University Professorship. He is the author of the memoirs *Planet of the Blind* (a New York Times "Notable Book of the Year") and *Eavesdropping: A Memoir of Blindness and Listening* and of the poetry collections *Only Bread, Only Light* and *Letters to Borges*. His newest memoir, *Have Dog, Will Travel: A Poet's Journey* is new from Simon & Schuster. A graduate of the Iowa Writer's Workshop and a

Fulbright Scholar, he has taught at the University of Iowa, Hobart &
William Smith Colleges, and The Ohio State University. Professor
Kuusisto has served as an advisor to the Metropolitan Museum
and the Museum of Modern Art in New York and the National
Endowment for the Arts in Washington DC and has appeared on
numerous television and radio programs including The Oprah
Winfrey Show; Dateline; All Things Considered; Morning Edition;
Talk of the Nation; A & E; and Animal Planet. His essays have
appeared in The New York Times; The Washington Post; Harper's;
The Reader's Digest; and his daily blog "Planet of the Blind" is read
globally by people interested in disability and contemporary culture.
He is a frequent speaker in the US and abroad. His website is: www.
stephenkuusisto.com

Paul E Nelson

Paul Nelson is a poet & interviewer. He founded SPLAB (Seattle
Poetics LAB) & the Cascadia Poetry Festival. Since 1993, SPLAB
has produced hundreds of poetry events & 600 hours of interview
programming with legendary poets, indigenous people & whole
systems activists. Paul's books include *American Prophets* (interviews
1994-2012) (2018) *American Sentences* (2015) *A Time Before Slaughter*
(2009) and *Organic in Cascadia: A Sequence of Energies* (2013). Co-
Editor of *Make It True: Poetry From Cascadia, 56 Days of August: Poetry
Postcards* and *Make it True meets Medusario* (2019) he's engaged in a
20 year bioregional cultural investigation of Cascadia, serves as Sam
Hamill's Literary Executor and lives in Rainier Beach, in the Cascadia
bioregion's Cedar River watershed. www.PaulENelson.com.

William O'Daly

William O'Daly has translated eight books of the late-career
and posthumous poetry of Chilean Nobel laureate Pablo Neruda,
and most recently Neruda's first volume, *Book of Twilight,* a finalist
for the 2018 Northern California Book Award in Translation. All
nine Neruda translations are published by Copper Canyon Press.
O'Daly's books of poems include *The Whale in the Web,* also published
by Copper Canyon, as well as *The Road to Isla Negra* (2015), *Water*

Ways (2017, a collaboration with JS Graustein), and *Yarrow and Smoke* (2018), the latter three published by Folded Word Press. A National Endowment for the Arts Fellow, O'Daly was a finalist for the 2006 Quill Award in Poetry and was profiled by Mike Leonard for *The Today Show*. A three-time Pushcart Prize nominee, his poems, translations, essays, and reviews have been published in numerous journals and as part of multimedia exhibits and performances. His essay "Creative Collisions: Poetry as a Transformative Act" was a finalist for Tiferet Journal's 2018 Writing Contest. He has received national and regional honors for literary editing and instructional design, was a co-founder of Copper Canyon Press, and served on the board of Poets Against War. Most recently, he was awarded by the State of California for his written and editorial contributions to the California Water Plan.

Thomas Hitoshi Pruiksma

Thomas Hitoshi Pruiksma is an author, poet, translator, teacher, magician, musician, and lover of life. He was born in Seattle, has worked in south India and southern Mexico, and is currently a 2018-2019 NEA Translation Fellow. Earlier this year, Marrowstone Press published his first collection of poems, *The Safety of Edges*. Other books include *Give, Eat, and Live: Poems of Avvaiyar* and *Body and Earth* (with the artist C.F. John). Pruiksma performs nationally and internationally, and serves as Language Consultant for the Cozy Grammar Series of Video Courses. He makes his home on Vashon Island with his husband, David Mielke. thomaspruiksma.com

Heidi Seaborn

Heidi Seaborn is the author of the award-winning debut book of poetry *Give a Girl Chaos {see what she can do}* (C&R Press/Mastodon Books, March 2019), Editorial Director for *The Adroit Journal* and a New York University MFA candidate. Since Heidi started writing in 2016, she's won or been shortlisted for nearly two dozen awards including the International Rita Dove Award in Poetry and published in numerous journals and anthologies such as *The Missouri Review, Mississippi Review, Penn Review* and *Nimrod*, as well a chapbook and a political pamphlet. She graduated from Stanford University and is on the board of Tupelo Press. heidiseabornpoet.com

Rebecca Seiferle

Rebecca Seiferle is the author of four poetry collections. Her most recent collection *Wild Tongue* (Copper Canyon Press, 2007) won the 2008 Grub Street National Poetry Prize. In 2004 she was awarded the Lannan Literary Fellowship for poetry. She has published two book length translations of César Vallejo: *Trilce* (Sheep Meadow Press, 1992) and *The Black Heralds* (Copper Canyon, 2003). Her translations are also included in *The Whole Island: Six Decades of Cuban Poetry* (University of California Press, 2009) and *Reversible Monuments: Contemporary Mexican Poetry* (Copper Canyon, 2001). She was Tucson Poet Laureate from 2012–16.

Karma Tenzing Wangchuk

Karma Tenzing Wangchuk (Dennis H. Dutton) is the author of several poetry chapbooks including *90 Frogs, Stone Buddha* and *Shelter | Street: Haiku & Senryu.* A Los Angeles native, Tenzing has lived in Port Townsend, Cascadia, since 2006.